Dinosaur Detectives
Search for the facts...

Moschops
and Other
Ancient Reptiles

Tracey Kelly

raintree

a Capstone company — publishers for children

Raintree is an imprint of Capstone Global Library Limited, a company incorporated in England and Wales having its registered office at 264 Banbury Road, Oxford, OX2 7DY – Registered company number: 6695582

www.raintree.co.uk
myorders@raintree.co.uk

Text: Tracey Kelly
Designer: John Woolford
Design Manager: Keith Davis
Editorial Director: Lindsey Lowe
Children's Publisher: Anne O'Daly
Picture Manager: Sophie Mortimer
Production by Katy LaVigne
Printed and bound in India

ISBN 978 1 4747 7829 9 (hardback)
ISBN 978 1 4747 7835 0 (paperback)

British Library Cataloguing in Publication Data
A full catalogue record for this book is available from the British Library.

Acknowledgements
We would like to thank the following for permission to reproduce photographs:
Public Domain: Granger 4.

Every effort has been made to contact copyright holders of material reproduced in this book. Any omissions will be rectified in subsequent printings if notice is given to the publisher.

Contents

How do we know about dinosaurs?

Scientists are like detectives.
They look at fossils.
Fossils tell us where dinosaurs and other
ancient reptiles lived.
They tell us how big they were.

Robert Broom was
a dinosaur detective.
He found *Moschops* fossils
in 1910. He found them
in South Africa. *Moschops*
had a thick skull. People
guessed that it used
its head to fight.

How to use this book

This tells you what the animal ate.

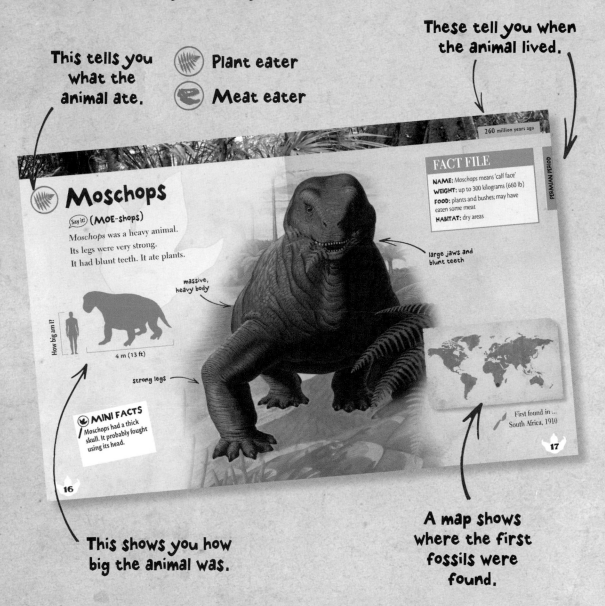

🌿 Plant eater

🦖 Meat eater

These tell you when the animal lived.

260 million years ago

PERMIAN PERIOD

🌿 **Moschops**

Say it! **(MOE-shops)**

Moschops was a heavy animal.
Its legs were very strong.
It had blunt teeth. It ate plants.

massive, heavy body

How big am I?

4 m (13 ft)

strong legs

🌿 **MINI FACTS**
Moschops had a thick skull. It probably fought using its head.

FACT FILE

NAME: Moschops means 'calf face'
WEIGHT: up to 300 kilograms (660 lb)
FOOD: plants and bushes; may have eaten some meat
HABITAT: dry areas

large jaws and blunt teeth

First found in ...
South Africa, 1910

16

17

This shows you how big the animal was.

A map shows where the first fossils were found.

Read on to become a dinosaur detective!

What was Earth like?

Moschops lived in the Permian period.
That was millions of years ago.
Earth was very dry. Plants grew near water
pools. Ancient reptiles ate and drank there.

Bradysaurus

Say it! (BRAY-dee-SAW-rus)

Bradysaurus had a huge body. It had strong limbs. Its head had bony ridges. Its teeth were shaped like leaves.

head 'crown' made of bony ridges

MINI FACTS

Bradysaurus moved slowly. It was clumsy! The turtle might be related to it!

FACT FILE

NAME: *Bradysaurus*
means 'Brady's lizard'
or 'slow reptile'

WEIGHT: up to 1 tonne
(1 ton)

FOOD: plants

HABITAT: large swamps

How big am I?

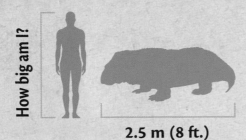

2.5 m (8 ft.)

big body

hard scales

short, strong limbs

First found in ...
South Africa, 1914

9

Coelurosauravus

Say it! (SEEL-your-oh-SAW-rave-us)

Coelurosauravus looked like a lizard with wings! Each wing had 22 tiny bones. These were covered with skin. *Coelurosauravus* could glide in the air.

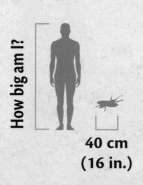

How big am I?

40 cm
(16 in.)

long head with frill

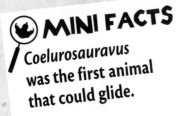

MINI FACTS

Coelurosauravus was the first animal that could glide.

long tail
helped flight

FACT FILE

NAME: *Coelurosauravus* means 'hollow-tipped reptile bird'

WEIGHT: about 0.5 kg (1 lb.)

FOOD: insects in the trees

HABITAT: woodland in Germany, England and Madagascar

lizard-like legs

wings opened like a fan

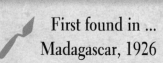

First found in ...
Madagascar, 1926

Dicynodon

Say it! (dye-SINE-oh-don)

Dicynodon had a bulky body, a bit like a pig.
It had strong legs. Its large teeth could break
off plants.

horny beak, used
to bite plants

FACT FILE

NAME: *Dicynodon* means 'two dog-teeth'

WEIGHT: 11 kg (24 lbs.)

FOOD: plants and roots

HABITAT: most lived on land, but a few lived in the water

How big am I?

1.2 m (4 ft.)

pig-like body shape

MINI FACTS

Dicynodon lived in groups. This kept it safe from meat eaters.

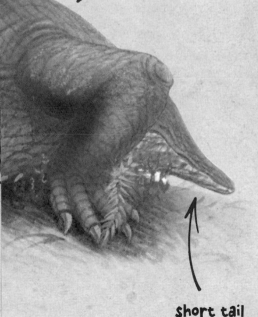

short tail

First found in ...
South Africa, 1845

13

Dinosaur quiz

Test your dinosaur detective skills!
Can you answer these questions?
Look in the book for clues.
The answers are on page 24.

What kind of teeth
did *Bradysaurus* have?
What did it eat?

Which dinosaur lived
near swamps, lakes
and coasts?

Why did *Dimetrodon*
have a sail on its back?

Was *Euparkeria* a fast
or slow runner?

Glossary

fossil
Part of an animal or plant in rock.
The animal or plant lived in ancient times.

habitat
The kind of place where an animal usually lives.

herd
A group of animals that lives together.

meat eater
An animal that eats mostly meat.

plant eater
An animal that eats only plants.

prey
An animal that is hunted
by other animals for food.

Triassic period
The time that
came after the
Permian period.

Find out more

Books

National Geographic Little Kids First Big Book of Dinosaurs, Catherine D. Hughes (National Geographic Kids, 2011)

The Big Book of Dinosaurs, DK Editors (DK Children, 2015)

Websites

www.bbc.co.uk/sn/prehistoric_life/dinosaurs

www.natgeokids.com/uk/play-and-win/games/dinosaur-memory

www.nhm.ac.uk/discover/dino-directory

Index

Quiz answers: 1. *Bradysaurus* had leaf-shaped teeth. It ate plants. **2.** *Lystrosaurus.* **3.** The sail helped *Dimetrodon* to soak up heat from the sun. **4.** It was a fast runner.